Not Your Average Fairytale Poetry & Prose

Rachel Wylie

Kelly,
Thank you for believing in me!

Kelli,
Thank you for believing in me!

Not Your Average Fairytale

Not Your Average Fairytale, Copyright © 2023 by Rachel Wylie

All rights reserved.

No part of this book may be reproduced, distributed, or transmitted in any
form or by any means including electronic, mechanical, photocopying, recording,
or otherwise without the consent from the copyright owner.

Cover Art by Kelly Emmrich
Editing and Formatting by Maggie Bowyer
Poems by Rachel Wylie

First Printing, 2023
ISBN 979-8-9889100-0-8

Not Your Average Fairytale

Dear Reader,

I wouldn't be here without you believing in me.
My voice has a chance because of you.
It means so much more to me than I will ever be
able to truly express.
I'm beyond excited to gift this to you all.
Here's to many more stories yet to be told.

Table of Contents

Part 1: The Wallflower 9

    Freshman Year: 11

    Sophomore Experience: 19

    Junior Shutout: 25

    Senior Fever Dream: 33

Part 2: Contusions from a Boy 39

    Convicted: 41

    Bitter: 51

    Insecure: 61

    Painful Truth: 71

Part 3: The Stars 77

    The Irrational Phase: 79

    Challenging the Thinking: 87

    Cut Short: 97

Part 4: Everytime 103

    Chills: 105

It'll be Ok: 115

Motions in and Out: 123

Playback: 133

Part 1: The Wallflower

Freshman Year

First Week

Deception misguiding the lines
Swerving down unfamiliar roads
The signs hit hard

Shock sends my body shivering
Seasick from swaying
Floating 6 feet above

A choked personality
Keeping my mouth sewn shut,
The fear of rejection
Paralyzing my brain

Polaroid

Breathing quickens as you're frozen in this dream
Sitting in the back corner of class
Peeling the layers of paint
Off your number 2 golden pencil
Stale stiffness circles the air
Delicately repeating the number
Of people before you
Rehearsing the lines shaking in black ink

That feeling erupts
A true jump scare it seems
It zaps your blood
Boiling it into gas
The chaotic fearful thoughts
Slap you across the face
Kicking aside all logic

No matter what escapes your mouth
Their piercing painful laughter
Will pull all air from your lungs
How embarrassing it is
Stuttering through a paragraph
You're at the age where they'll mock you indeed
Hands sticky and soaked

Daggers dig into your vocal cord
Chills wrap you in foil
Your name's been uttered
Voice weak
You ask for a pass

Not Your Average Fairytale

All eyes fall on you
Surrendering with a white flag
Instead of reading aloud
Leads to a disconnect from everyone else

INT. SUBURBAN BASEMENT – NIGHT

Booming voices outweigh musical tones
Cut low and lost in between
Foaming mineral waste
Splattered against the interior of the throat
Fog contributed by dense haze soaking up the air
Shoes suctioned to the ground below

Why did I think this was a good idea? I ask myself almost out of disgust

Pretending to be deeply invested in a conversation
With some sweaty, pimple-glazed, adolescent, axe body spray twig

This is what I'm *supposed to do*
This is the fun everyone talks about
A fundamental experience of growing up

Suck it up. Look like you're doing what everyone else is.

The anxiety pulsing, vibrating lungs, ringing ears, and shaking hands
It creeps up
Clogging the throat
Throwback another shot without hesitation
Feel that sticky syrupy burn dissolve all fears

After all, this **is** what fun is

FADE TO BLACK.

Ruminator

Thoughts pulling me out of this world
Consuming my brain
Freezing me in an alternate state
Eternally fearful of living outside of the mold

Sophomore Experience

Habits.

Anxiety gnawing
Ripping hunger to shreds.
Wasted off toxic breath.
Swallowed in a blurry state.
Overtaken by a villain.
Scarfing down all logic.
Tinting my perspective.
Consuming me in shame.

Trapped Inside

Sometimes I feel like a caged bird
Forgotten in the background
Feasting off whatever I can find
Until I run out for good

Soaked in Bleach

Never been one to look through rose-colored glasses
Eyes dried out
Bloodshot
Drained like a sponge

Suck it up out of convenience
An addict to the obsessions
Rarely satisfied by compulsions

The stress of it all
The temporary relief of it all
Ignites craving like no other
Patterns raise the tolerance
Leaving an itch impossible not to scratch

Soak in bleach to sterilize freckles
Glue to an obsessive skincare routine to avoid creases
Eat less and exercise vigorously for a flatter stomach
Internalize disgust.
Discomfort.
Distortions.
Clog arteries with compliments.

Laugh at the nature of it all.

Ignore the reality of it all.

Misunderstood

The most beautiful souls
Tend to undergo
Years of torment
Scratched up the waist
In order to shine so bright
The stars idolize them

Not Your Average Fairytale

Junior Shutout

Wasteful Youth

I'm told to celebrate this time of life.

But I've never felt like more of an imposter.

Loathing every second

Faking the biggest smile

I love -

Fragile hearts
Cling tight
Casually loving
Playing hard to get for fucks sake
Passionately misleading down hopeless trails
Until the chord falls off key
The boredom strikes your tone
The pauses increase
Your reservations overshadow your reasons

                                      I miss the red flags
                                      And end up thinking
                                      You're the best thing
                                      To ever happen

You pull back.
I face plant.
Time moves on.
We don't.

                                      Chills creep up
                                      Replacing your hands
                                      I cling tightly
                                      To an overly
                                      Romanticized idea:

You'll call in a couple of months
Say how the past several
Have been the worst ones yet

Not Your Average Fairytale

                        You need me
                        More than ever

But you never do.

                        I'm left staring
                        At my ceiling

Wondering why love cuts off mid-sentence

Popular Kids

Gallantly awaiting
        The death of a sailor
In a fog of amber and gray
        The host of the funeral
Battered and brave
        Led the endeavor
Down a cauldron
        Makeshift and stray
Deeply in vain

Fearfully Fearless

The freckles across your face
Leave me in a state of grace
I'm caught off guard
By the thought of you keeping me up
These daydreams have me questioning a lot

Between The Lines

The rope keeping me from falling is fraying

Moments this close to the drop
Cause my breathing to shake
I'm more unsteady than ever before,
Heart squeezing from the pressure
Of my own hands

Slipping as we speak
What will happen if I let go?

I once wrote down a thought
About hanging onto a branch
Off the edge of a cliff

Yet I was only 2 feet from the ground
But distortions misguided my brain

I know this drop is further
And it's going to hurt
If I don't land on my feet

Senior Fever Dream

Social Media Isolation

Silkscreens mask the drama
Drenched in the background
Floating in & out of focus
Light-headed from your shove
On the verge of losing all balance
Abandoned
Left to rot
Scream into the void
Hoping it will solve
The tear in my heart

Essay 1

I've spent most nights wondering about you. I know I don't know you yet, sure. It doesn't keep me from thinking… Dreaming, really. You're off somewhere else. In another land. Living a life we'll soon talk about as memories. I have expectations about you of course, but I've learned the universe loves to throw curve balls.

We have absolutely no control over the people we fall in love with. Yet, there's an entire crowd out there bickering about men (they don't know) kissing other men. Meanwhile, they cheer as soon as they see two women make out in a bar. Fuck double standards.

For the Love of Poetry

Poetry is a drug
For the ones who struggle
To silence their minds
In the oddest of hours

Universal Nightmare

You wake.
Alone.
Tucked away in your dark empty bedroom.
Drenched in sweat.
Only to discover
It's another Thursday
And you're only 18.
In the middle of a global pandemic.
America is consumed by a full mental breakdown.
Leaving us
As paranoid and anxious as possible.

- Just suck up the pain and down another shot of pickle juice

Part 2: Contusions From a Boy

Not Your Average Fairytale

Convicted

Mars

a parasite crawled its way inside my brain
devouring its essence
sucking it bone dry
healthy tissue
becoming cracked, fragile.
sugar coating it with dark matter
wishes morphing into fears
until everything is eventually unrecognizable
and i've somehow become an alien to my own story

Love Story

Blankly staring at the ground
Tethered to a park bench
The last piece of the puzzle
Vanished with zero trace

You're long gone
My heart cries
Who am I supposed to turn to
When all I want

Is the idea
Of you

Plague

If we all fall
Bury me in a casket
So mismanaged, pathetic, fragile
Just enough
So, the universe
Can sit back and laugh

Left in The Air

The wonders of your voice
Leave me shivering
Chilled by staleness
Wound so tight
I'm plastered off insecurities
Tangled up in meaningless phrases

I can't help but fall off key.
You want me to be something I can't.
Something I'm not.

I'm wasted off your false promises
The ones I know will leave me hurting the most

Strung out on dialectics
Praying reality might somehow drag me off screen
Outside of a spotlight

Save Yourself, Love

I've been thinking a lot about myself as a kid
The way things were so much easier
Life hadn't started laughing yet
I hadn't met you
Hadn't spent nights crying myself to sleep
Didn't know how earth-shattering heartbreak is
Hadn't experienced heartless breakup methods
I wasn't looked at as an object
You never sent mixed signals
I wasn't difficult yet
Nothing haunted my bones

Once you finally ended it
In the most impersonal way possible
I'm reminded
Love's never the way it's portrayed in the movies

Gaslight

Can you love the version of me
That wants to numb my heart
Because the sorrow is smothering

I've suffocated long enough
To know only a ventilator
Can give my lungs a second chance
I'm haunted by the traumas of my past
It kills me
How long I've stumbled in the dark

It was never in your heart to love me
I wish I had the ability to stop thinking
About the girl you'll hold and kiss into the night
That's not me

Pov

Heart crumbles within
The memories flash before my eyes
A smile torn   replaced by a frown
The tears flood
In a way they haven't been able to in years
I thought we possessed something special
Yet here I am   strung out
        On your love.
I completely lost control
            Of my story

Bitter

Purgatory

Dancing high above the clouds
Three months shy of a year
I dreamt about you every night
I thought I needed everything we were

Now you're just etched into my skull
I can't stop circling and replaying
The drama in the last things you said
To know it all ended before I was ready

What if one thing had been different?
What if I'd met you a year from now?
Could we have made it a lifetime?
Were we too different to last?

I wish I could read thoughts

Because only hearing myself

Is driving me straight off the edge

The end.

Collapsing to my knees
Throbbing
Soaked in blood
Time slipped through my fingers
It's my funeral
And you didn't bother to show

Stuck

Strolling down an abandoned street
Muttering the million reasons
Why I'm never a good enough partner
And always end up on my own

Dodging Love

Fearful of love
I've been hiding behind a disguise
Afraid of being direct and open
Disappearing in the wind
Leaving no trace

Primed History

I harmonize a broken tone
Crystalized as a fossil
Locked in a sandbox

Lonely Girl

Wandering through streets
Late into the night
Ghosts call out my name
Their voices echo
Haunted by broken hearts
Bouncing off abandoned buildings
Full of stories forgotten long ago
Never to be shared

Love Conspiracy

The funeral to our love
Dried out my tears
And carried me off screen
I floated for what felt like years

Chasing your voice
You continued to walk away
As if I was a passing thought
You could block out

Insecure

Yellow Wallpaper

If I lived a life with no mirrors
Would you tell me
I'm everything

The reflection I see
Mocks me
Plays tricks on me
Sizes everything up disproportionally
Tells me to cut off pieces of flesh
And donate them to the walls
That never answer

Headbanger

I harmonize a broken fate
Tossing me scraps for a century
My mind becoming more like putty
With each shaking breath
Your voice lingers in my head
Repeating the same few words
I wish you never uttered

Your escape
Ran over my heart
Shattering it into pieces
The fate of us
Was never meant to last
I bite my tongue
Hoping to numb the inside of my mouth

Your tone couldn't have morphed quicker
And it didn't even phase you
I wish there was another universe
Where our differences didn't drive you mad
And straight out the door
Our relationship turned into a dead end
Marked with no sign

Dead Poet

I tossed a stone in the water
It didn't skip
It sunk
Deep
And
Fast
      Just as the weight of us

            Left me drowning

Part of me knows

      I only loved the idea

Of you.

Mind's Antidepressant

Anxiety's been eating me alive most of my life
I can't seem to get it out of my head
The ache of the past, present, and future
Swarm me in a fever state
Surrounded by the worst dull pain
To occupy
My massive, empty heart

Shakespeare Tragedies in The Modern Era

You stabbed me in the chest
Loving the tear
It created
Drenching my soul
In gooey, clumpy syrup

Lead me on
Until you're waist deep
In pocket change
Frustrated by my existence

Blank

Medication should lessen the blunt force trauma

Yet

You always
Find a way
To bash my head in

Mental Burn Book

The clowns and circus freaks swarm my head
Pointing, laughing,
Calling me a brainless piece of shit
I sit in front of a blank screen trying to escape
From this world of ridicule
In hopes of saving myself

Expiration Date

Love always feels timeless
    The moment it takes off…
        Blindly unaware

            Of its terminal expiration date.

Painful Truth

Candy in the Backseat of a Strangers Car

The hesitation in my tone
Leaves my belly shaking
My breath stuttering at the speed of light

I envy you.
You block me out.
The horoscope was a load of bullshit.

You talk at me
Falsely understanding
Your words burn through the air

And just like that
I learned
You never even knew me in the first place

Coming of Age

I've spent most of my youth
Focusing on what makes me empty
And the people who've crushed me
Rather than embracing
The things and people
That make me feel whole

All Tricks and No Treats

It's only been a few weeks
Since I've stopped sleeping in your bed;
I remember turning over to kiss your forehead as
you slept.

I remember feeling like the luckiest person.
I think I latched onto a reality
That was never meant to last more than 9 months.

How was I so utterly oblivious to your reservations?
I think it's because of the way you used to say you
loved me
It felt so tangible.

Essay 2

Dear You,
You found me when I was broken
I think my biggest mistake
Was making You the one to piece me back together
I've never been able to figure out why I flock
towards the ones who never get it
Love hurts the most
When one's been naïve enough to buy into it
You said to my face,
> *People never change*

I think deep down I knew we'd never work
So why did I choose to ignore it?
There was an expiration date on our love
In a way that'd lead you to vanish for eternity
With no trace
Shoving me off a ledge
Abruptly
Confused
And forgotten

Part 3:
The Stars

The Irrational Phase

Prison

Drowning in it all
I feel so far away
My voice never sounds
I still try to scream anyway

Alone
Surrounded by a prison of walls
There are faces on the ceiling
Mocking and laughing away

They act like they know everything
But only know my name
It's a terrible mess
The situation I'm in

I've got an unreliable label super glued to my forehead
It's placed me in a terrible mess you see
Any slight deviation from normal
Pushes me outside of the box

I don't want to be a centerfold
I don't want a forced responsibility
I don't want to stand out

My heart's been toyed with
Forcing me to say
The one thing
I'm not ready to

Let me Tell you Something

Pop culture has taught us above all else
To feel uncomfortable
And think exclusively in stereotypes
Whenever it comes to **The Gays.**

We hear on repeat:
Gayness *isn't natural.*
It's a defeat.
It's a reason to abandon family members.
It's disgusting.
It's embarrassing.
It's unacceptable.
It should only exist as a fetish in pornography.

They'll tell you to clog up **Gay** thoughts
And soak in shame
Heteronormativity teaches us
Above all personalities
Above all dreams
Above all life accomplishments
You're **Gay.**

Whatever insults come to mind
Let them out
Shove concrete down throats
Evaporate organically driven attraction
Kiss the opposite sex praying it won't leave you numb
Control the clothes you wear on your back

Become a plot point in a TV show for the sake of added views
Only for them to express the wrong narrative
Control the story you share
Or bear the risk of rejection
And peer driven labels

Let's face it.
It feels easier staying quiet
You don't want to be a part of the punchline
When your High School peers get together
And talk about who turned out **Gay** for shock value.

They'll question interactions they had with you
Were the signs always there?
According to them,
You had a crush on so and so
Because you were nice that one time and well…look how you turned out
It doesn't matter if your interactions were awkward
Because you happened to be awkward in High School

They don't look at it that way
To them
You'll never be more
Then just **Gay.**

Binaries

Compliments leave my stomach in knots
Tangled so tight I turn sour
When they come from men, anything
But gentle.

They'd say things to perk up my ego
Only to tear it down behind my back
He said things that made me want to stay "straight"

Queer labels always slap you across the face
In the most impersonal way
The chances of rejection are high
The fear builds up
The walls cave in

People are going to call you out
And say being Bi or Pan
Is a fast-track transition
To a full-blown gay translation

Internet Kid

In the minute of time
You can meet someone
Get to talking
Fall in love
Grow bored
Ghost
Become strangers
Move on like they never existed

- Sometimes I hate my generation

Essay 3

I've tried to write this 10 dozen times and have failed with every attempt / The room's always spinning / I can hardly keep food down / My foot never seems to quit ending up in my mouth / Uttering the words, dancing around my mind, coating my lungs in fear / I'm an imposter to my own world / Putting others before me, while ignoring my own needs / It's all become second nature it seems / There's a level of rejection owning up to my sexuality / The way loved one's misinterpret the signs / The way they permanently tattoo a label to my forehead / The way they try to steer me away from making *that* mistake / I realize most of this fear lingering in my mind is not validated / But it's nearly impossible not letting the anticipation get the best of me

Challenging the Thinking

Caving in

You're nothing like I ever could have imagined
Taking up a piece of my brain
Once filled with regret and shame
The weight finally feels bearable
And it's all because
I have you to thank with that sweet smile and soft brown eyes

Thinking in Color

I'm walking into a movie
Experiencing color for the first time

I can't stop smiling
And it's all because of you

Faint Reality

I asked the universe when I'd meet the man of my dreams
      Alas, No one answered
I proceeded to ask once again hoping the outcome would change
      Although, the universe shrugged…not knowing what else to say
I felt my lungs filling with a scream
      And just like that
      I was greeted by a tap on my shoulder
As soon as I turned around… I was greeted by you and that smile

Darling
Love works in the oddest of ways
We attempt to control its pull
Only to be let down when we try to shape love forcefully
The universe teaches us relentlessly with lessons
Shattering our hearts when it's truly unrealistic
Taunting us until our vision turns gray

I met you in the middle of a covid time warp
Playing the oddest of games
Unrealistically expecting the most
There's no way this makes it
I know I'm going to end up bruised
But it doesn't keep me from praying
This is all the real deal.

Penciled in For Tuesday

Your eyes say it all
You're looking at me like no one's ever
My throat's clogged with speech
While lyrical wine pours from your mouth

    -   I couldn't be drunker off you

Predicted Endings

I thought he brought me utter happiness for months
Yet, I'd always hold my breath   *in a negligent way*
Love isn't supposed to dress you up in anxiety

I replay the memories off a projector
The closer we got, the more I shut down
Flinch whenever we'd kiss
Dread every phone call
Speaking my mind felt like too much of a chore

And then I think of her
How I'm left singing whenever texts fill my lock screen
How we lose track of time talking on the phone for hours
How nerves crossed with excitement consume my entire being whenever we meet up

I'm such a sucker for love
The act of falling
Not being able to think about anything else
The constant giddy energy
Losing track of speech patterns all because of eye contact

It no longer feels like work
All I want is for this to last
A lifetime

Changes

There's a version of us
One where we aren't ridiculed
For being our real selves

I want to take up a piece of your brain
So anytime my name shoots across your screen
You can't help but flutter & sing

Fillers

My mind's no longer empty
I never saw this coming
I'm dancing high above the clouds
Petrified of getting cut short and falling face first

Cut Short

Heartbreak

It isn't supposed to leave you gasping…
Love, that is.

So tell me…
How did I ever make it to this point
Where holding my breath for 5 seconds too long
feels blissful?

The red flags burn like acid,
My heart's tied together in knots,
She hesitates because she's never been in love.
I tell myself
It's all normal really…

- How some people walk into your life
  And initiate I love you
  With no intentions of ever sticking around

Rumination Relapse

Your face spins around my memories
I hate how I can't stop writing about you
Loves always scared me
How fragilely constructed it ends up being
The pain feels fake when someone takes a vacuum to your heart

Reject my soul
Regurgitate it on a table
Taunt me online
Disappear in thin air

All while I can't stop singing your name.

Undrunk

You're always in the back of my dreams

Morning's rise

My mind tricks me

Into believing

You still want me

I have to unlearn you

As my muse
As my person
As my confidant
As the person I'd run to with any kind of news

I have to learn to let you go.
I have to learn to stop checking in on you
I have to stop overthinking why it never worked

I hate how I get caught up in this spiral
How you perceived me at my lowest.
I wish I could just ~~let it all~~ let you go.

Part 4: Everytime

Chills

Not Your Average Fairytale

So high & low
To states untold
Forget the things I said
Which dragged you off the ledge

Toxic Waste

On a juice cleanse
Detoxing you from my lungs.
Those clothes no longer burn a stain in the corner of my room
They're stacked neatly in the back of my closet
Never to grace my skin again
They remind me too much of you.

You claimed they were the reason you chose to hollow out my heart
Piercing the most painful holes in my chest
I used to love your toxicity

Now…
You're everything I hate.

Angel Baby

I watched the sky fold inward last night
Hoping you'd appear
The second the sun began to poke its way over the horizon

Flashes from another life
Swarmed my conscious state
I lay with you in bed, sleeping still

We first met on a Thursday night
You downed some wine beforehand
Because your anticipatory anxiety left you seeing spots

- I dream about you in ways that'll never
  Cause the poetry to stop flowing

Misfit

I sit atop a counter in the corner of this college loft
Densely covered by sludge
Concocted by beer, mud, cigarette smoke, and sweat
Sipping on a slightly stale room temperature natty light
Fuckin College

Some tall athlete jumps into the open space next to me
His cologne overpowering the boundaries of my nose
Leaving me wanting to gag
Overflowing my throat with bile
Sup.

By society standards, he's considered attractive
I find him rather bland
He talks at me for what feels like an hour
About his Business Major
How he's always wanted to go into banking for the money
How he and his teammates got plastered
And completely trashed a hotel room in Vail
How original.

I couldn't be more distracted
By two girls kissing
Across the room
Unafraid of what others will shout

Not Your Average Fairytale

Good for them.

Depressed as hell
Hiding behind a faceless mask
I'm lost in my thoughts
Contemplating the real me
Is she even achievable?
Probably not.

Days lost ruminating
Over how I'm perceived
How others act
How I think I should act
I want to be liked
So, I'll cremate myself to fit social standards
Lose myself in the process
Learn to hate my name.
The words leave my mouth
Before I even realize their extent
I turn to the guy, ask him if he wants to get out of here
It feels like the right thing to do
I fuckin hate this.

Pity

You shattered my heart
I grew to resent myself
Until every inch of my body
Fell stiff
Covered in scales

Dear John

I've dreamed of us and where we've gone
Matches ignited the fire to our fate
You vanished
I searched high and low
Always ended up empty handed

I cleaned up the mess you left my heart in
Even told myself it was all my fault
Your love overshadowed my voice
Anything I ever said, was never enough or right
Somewhere along the way, I lost myself

You became so fixated on not gaslighting…
It's all you ever did
I fell in love
In the most miserable way possible

It took you walking out in the most impersonal way
For me to finally feel thankful & reach peace

It'll be Ok

Alternate Ending

Once you're off dreaming
I'm over the moon, unable to sleep, unstable with time
I can't get you out of my head
You tattooed yourself so deeply to my chest

I thought this book would be a gift for you.
Slowly, look how the times changed
Meanings morphed
You grew drier in my memory

The heart of the text showed me what I had been missing
Fear driven thoughts striped my brain
Igniting insecurities on the spot
Codependently living off misfit energy

In some ways you still hold a deep core grip on some of the themes
Trying to figure out how to talk about you
Led me down a road of self-discovery
All without you to walk me there

For a long time
I got really good at perfectly digging my own grave
Overcompensating became second nature
Because I felt like an outcast

Look where we ended up.
So much time has gone by

I've wasted so much of it
Trying to piece together a meaning

The text in bold font in front of me.
You couldn't look beyond your own scars
So much so you played them out with mine
Until it got too close to real

I should have known.
I was always going to be your secret.
That led me to hold my breath for years.
You wanted to love me on your own timeline.

Tuesday Nights

For the first time
I'm done spending my life endlessly sleeping
Still a little emotionally raw around the edges
My tongue speaks in a way that once made me mute

Someone New

I sit here
On my bed
Sipping some wine
Attempting to develop a character
For a project
I've been writing, deleting, writing
On an endless time loop

I can't get you out of my head
The latest distraction to my mind and heart
You're so new
So how do I know everything
Your starstruck blue eyes
Reveal a scarred past
Splashed with the greatest humor

You leave me speechless
Constantly rehearsing conversations in my head
We'll never have
You're a temporary placeholder in my heart
You keep me at arm's reach
On a long enough leash so once you drop me

You won't hear me smack into the earth
It's bittersweet
You've never been one to linger
I'd love to know you better
It'll never pan out
At the end of the day
The fall doesn't sting as intensely

Not Your Average Fairytale

- You showed me
It's possible to move on from past heartache
And fall in love again

Strawberries
And wine
Hand in mine
Stars in the sky
Butterflies inside

Motions in and Out

Addict

Mistakes were made
I thrived off the self-destruction
Anything to keep my head above water
While slowly ending my demise

Other Side of the Universe

I thought I knew myself
Sitting down with my thoughts for a year
Proved me wrong
Perched here in the middle of the night, writing poetry
Has me discovering a new version
I don't want to place on hold anymore

I thought it'd be impossible for me to find someone
I'd fear losing
But here I am
At 1:30
Unable to sleep
Because you're always on my mind

Ticking

On a deep, dark, spiral
My mind flatlined
Temporarily

I learned the hard way
My story wasn't over
I just needed a hard reset

Dreams

The universe thrives off creating chaos:
I often find myself
Tripping over the what ifs that never pan out
The destruction that rarely occurs
I normalize obsessing over my tongue to an unhealthy degree
Praying it'll bring me to a balanced state

The light at the end of the tunnel
Sometimes feels millions and millions of miles away
But you grab my hand, leading me into the unknown
And for the first time
I'm ok not knowing what happens next

Cinderella

I attempted to harmonize a broken tone for months
Assuming a tune might catch
If I switched my pitch just right
The thinking patterns all seemed black and white

Prince Charming loved his false promises
Tangled up in short phrases
Told me my overthinking
Was redundant

But in the end
He pinned it at the reason
To grow resentful

It hurts the most
When stories don't end in fairytales

Pages

Soaring into another state
Swarming by a kaleidoscope of fates
The highest I've ever been

Once chilled to the bone
No longer battered
Warmed to the core

Fearless
Well… kind of…
The book's been written
The next one's yet
To be more than a passing thought

Not Your Average Fairytale

I've spent my life pouring my soul onto the page
Anticipation of a world unknown
Sweeping me off my toes

Playback

Sweater Weather

Damn December
You've always got me wanting love
Blue eyes and all
I stutter repeatedly

Looking at you
Totally unaware
Of your own potential
It's astonishing

I can't tell if I envy you
Because I wish I <u>was you</u>
    or
Because I wish I <u>was with you</u>

Damn December,
You've got me in my head all over again

Creaking Walls

Silence
Hours passing
Peaceful in bursts
Eerie in strides
Every night
You pray it won't be as bad as the last
And just like that
You're back in that moment
Consumed by a wave of trauma
The repetition in thinking changes nothing
Other than how you choose to isolate yourself
The loop gets old
Breaking the cycle is more of a chore
Nights linger
You're stuck in that collapsing room
Staring in the mirror at the monster smiling back
The nights fade
Ghosts laugh
Tears fall
Isolation persists

January

Marked by the haze of dusk
The skies cry
I smile
As I sit here
And write about you

What About Me?

I think what hurts the most
Is when you realize what you had with that person
Was never built to last
The way you once thought the stars aligned
Only to be let down by the absence in their air
How your heart dissolved rapidly the moment consistency let go

But after all
You're going to say it was them
And not you
Whether or not that's true
It always feels so painfully personal
The way someone can go from being your everything
To nothing at all

Backstage
Time feels cruel
To know you're out there without me
To know you're going to move on
While I fade into your background
To know you're going to look for people
Who don't remind you of me

The thoughts burn through my skull
And I think it's what hurts the most

Essay 4

My dreams sting
Half the time they're occupied by someone I can't be with
And the other half by something so new, so fragile
My heart may drop.
Time heals wounds
Changes the way we view people from our past
Makes us anxious about how we may get treated in the future
There's a constant fear
Of things we can't control

What if we had complete reign over our own lives?
Would you pick the perfect route?

Or the one that left scars on your knees,
Turned you upside down,
And shaped you differently?

My rarity gave way to trepidation;
In a lot of ways that fear held me back
It took hold of my lungs and I gave in
I tried to shape my life in a way that'd make me ordinary
And grew miserably resentful in the process
It took meeting someone I was told never to look at
To drag me from this fear
Nothing about it was perfect
It burned bright
And crashed hard
I said things I regret

She kept me a secret, unable to be honest

Times shifted
I'm older
You linger less in my head

The story I tried to write
Wrote me instead.

The end.

Acknowledgments

I would love to thank my editor, Maggie Bowyer, especially. You've believed in this project since I first brought it to you in ways I never could have anticipated. Maggie, I'm so honored to have had the opportunity to work with you. You'll always find a friend and fan in me.

Secondly, thank you again to Kelly Emmrich for creating an absolutely breathtaking cover I get to treasure for the rest of my life.

I want to thank my family. I know my dreams are a bit more off the beaten path; you've all supported me and have had my back as I continue striving closer to all my aspirations. I love you so much.

To my Grandma Pearl Ann, the relationship we've created is something I will cherish forever. You've had so many positive impacts on my life in more ways than I can ever thank. You've provided me with so much strength over the years and have believed in me in ways I have struggled with at times. You make me strong. I'm a survival warrior, partly thanks to you.

Lastly, to my younger self, precisely at 17. I know the world feels uncertain, and you feel a little lost in your identity. I promise, sweet girl, your moment will come. I'm so proud of you. Just wait and see what you're going to become.

Not Your Average Fairytale

Email:theeparanoidwriter@gmail.com
Instagram: @the_paranoid_writer

Printed in the USA
CPSIA information can be obtained
at www.ICGtesting.com
LVHW020522050524
779269LV00004B/636